REVI

MW00909672

Poems Fu. ..._ ...~.y

"*Simple words, simple poetic style — profound truth! Parents should read these poems to their children and reflect on them together. A genuine tool to lay the foundation for catechesis.*"

— Sister Ann Shields, SGL
Internationally known evangelist and host of the daily inspirational radio program, 'Food for the Journey'

"**Poems for His Glory** *is a beautiful collection of God-inspired poetry. Tom Catalano's experiences as a faith-filled father permeate his rich stanzas. His love for God is evident as one imbibes his poems. His daughter Emma, a poet in her own right, contributes inspiring poetry from the heart of a woman growing in holiness on a journey of faith. The reader should expect to feel God's presence while reading poems that are truly expressions of faith.*"

— Rev. Malachi Van Tassell, T.O.R., Ph.D.
President, Saint Francis University, Loretto, PA

"*As God's people, our most fundamental challenge is to keep God at the center of our daily lives and the events and activities that are a part of those lives. In addition to prayer, Scripture, and worship, the reflection of others is many times very helpful in this regard. Poetry that is God-centered and faith-inspired is one of those extra gifts that God gives us on our journey through this life to help us see ordinary things through the eyes of faith. In this splendid and delightful collection, Tom and Emma Catalano keep us grounded in the realization of God's extraordinary presence in our ordinary lives.*"

— Rev. Anthony J. Legarski
Pastor, Saint Mary Church, Hollidaysburg, PA

ABOUT THE AUTHORS

Tom Catalano

This is Tom's eighth published book but the first entirely comprised of poems directly tied to faith and spirituality. He has read his work at schools, libraries, bookstores, and community events throughout the country. His poetry has appeared in both U.S. and Canadian magazines and newspapers. His short stories have appeared in science fiction anthologies. He is a liturgical reader, a member of the Knights of Columbus and volunteers his time with the American Rescue Workers - the local food bank in his community.

Emma Catalano

Emma is Tom's daughter and an accomplished author and prolific poet. Her articles have been published in college newspapers and websites. She is a liturgical reader, volunteers at the American Rescue Workers, and has worked as a Peer Minister while a student at Saint Francis University. This is her first book.

POEMS
FOR
HIS
GLORY

original faith-inspiring poems

by

tom catalano
&
emma catalano

Charlotte,
God
Bless!

Tom catalano

To Betty Ann Catalano, my mother,
who made sure I was raised knowing God

To Lynda Berry, Jacqueline Cicchetti,
and Dr. Thomas Castner

FIRST EDITION

Copyright © 2017

by Thomas E. Catalano and Emma L. Catalano

Note: Some Christmas poems in *Poems For His Glory* have appeared previously in other books by **tom catalano.**

Printed in the United States of America

ISBN 978-1-882646-09-8

Published by:
Wordsmith Books
P.O. Box 221, Hollidaysburg, PA 16648 USA
catalano.tom@gmail.com

CONTENTS

FOREWARD 7

I'm Thankful 8

Prayer 9

Hope 10

What God Gives 11

I Live 12

For These Things 13

Make Me A Rock 15

A Glass Of Faith 16

A Wish 18

How Close Is That? 19

God Is Kind And Merciful 21

Guardian Angel 25

Heaven 26

Every Morn 28

Father And Son 29

I'll Ask The Lord 32

A Father's Prayer 34

The Big Game (God Sends In His Son) 37

I Do Believe 41

When He Comes Back 43

Cornerstone 44

Use Me 45

● ● ●

I Am A Berry 47

Our Spirits Have Soared 49

A Cross To Bear 50

All In 52

No Voice 54

The Heart Of Love 55

Who You Are 57

Not Forgotten 58

Repaid 60

My Castle Of Stone 64

A Child's Christmas 67

The Night Before Jesus 68

God's Gift 71

Christmas Upon Us 72

The Wish List 74

What I Want For Christmas 77

The Innkeeper 78

The Gift Tag Tree 82

Holiday Blues 84

The Mission 86

On His Birthday 94

The Point 95

BOOK SUMMARIES 96

FOREWORD

"The concept of this book came to me during a moment of prayer when I asked God how I could best serve Him. He gave me a strong and clear feeling that I should gather my spiritual poems in one place and share them with others. I immediately went to work gathering my favorites. Some tell a story, some recreate a special moment, and some capture an emotion...but all reflect the love, caring, forgiveness, and majesty of God. They are all for His glory. I saw an opportunity to work on this project with my daughter Emma, who is also strongly faith-based. She contributed many wonderful poems, which only made this book better. We sincerely hope you enjoy our poems and that they entertain and/or inspire you. If one of our poems touches you in some positive way, know that it is because God helped us convey that thought or emotion. Lastly, our thanks to Sr. Ann Shields, Rev. Malachi Van Tassell, and Fr. Anthony Legarski for taking time out of their busy schedules to review this book. To you, the reader, we wish you all of God blessings."

— tom catalano

"Poetry for me is kind of like cooking. Sometimes I have to put an idea on the back-burner before I figure out where I want the poem, and the story, to go. Other times, I am so inspired, that the poem gets written in one fell swoop. Passion is something that cannot be contained and God has inspired me to write it down. God is incomprehensible, so it's impossible to truly understand or put into words the magnificence and mystery of our Lord. But God made the invisible AND the visible, which is how I experience God's glory, through the world around me. God touches me with an idea, a concept, or a story that needs to be unraveled, and that helps me to better understand God. I find myself most at peace when I offer my gifts and talents to the Lord to be used for His will. My hope for you, the reader, is that you keep an open mind and an open heart, and that the poems my father and I felt inspired to write, are able to touch your life and strengthen your relationship with God."

— emma catalano

I'm Thankful

I only need to speak

    I know that you will hear.

If I have a problem

    I know that you are near.

And when I need a friend

    and I am all alone

you are always with me

    at work or in my home.

Times I am discouraged

    and I don't have a clue

I say a little prayer

    and put my faith in you.

You provide me guidance

    sometimes you lead the way.

For these things I'm thankful

    each and every day.

tom catalano

Prayer

When I get down on my knees

I often ask the Lord to please

bless my family and my friends

but this is not where my prayer ends.

"Thanks," is what I like to say

at the end of a long day

for helping me to make it through

and that He'll help you make it too.

When you drop down to your knees

won't you ask the Lord to please

bless those who haven't figured out

that prayer is what it's all about.

tom catalano

Hope

There're times our lives are troubling,

confusing, or obscure.

Answers seem so hard to find

and nothing is for sure.

Uncertainty will fill our minds,

we wonder how we'll cope,

but one thing keeps us hanging on

— the goodness found in hope.

We hope that things get better

and progress we will see,

but prayer will help our hope

become reality.

At times life is a struggle

it seems like every day.

I'm sure that you'll find peace,

of this I'll hope and pray.

tom catalano

What God Gives

God gives us strength

when we don't think

we have any.

He gives us courage

when we don't know

we need any.

He gives us love

when we don't feel

we deserve any.

tom catalano

I Live

I believe because I live

and I live because of Him.

He came to us with just one thought

to forgive the world of sin.

The times could not be better

for Him to spread His word —

the times could not be worse

some hated what they heard.

He spread the word of God

and He spread the love of man.

I can say without a doubt

He made me who I am.

He has kept His promise

our sins He would forgive.

I'm alive because He died

— I believe because I live.

tom catalano

For These Things

It's for these things that I do pray,

    ten little things to make my day:

Healthy children everywhere

    who have enough to eat and wear.

The homeless have a place to stay

    that's warm and safe each night and day.

The sick are healed or have hope

    with strength from God that they can cope.

That there's an end to bigotry

    and only goodness that we see.

And that we all love one another

    every neighbor, parent, brother.

The hate that enemies are sharing

    can be replaced by real caring.

That unborn voices can be heard

    above the din of those deterred.

That evil finds no heart to dwell

    and stays forever down in hell. ● ● ●

That peace will reign and love abound

'til Jesus comes and he is crowned.

That every earthly person knows

the grace and power God bestows.

It's for these things that I do pray,

each and every single day.

tom catalano

Make Me a Rock

Make me a rock, oh Lord,
so nothing can get in.
Harden my heart so I am
impervious to sin.

Make me a sponge, oh Lord,
to soak in all I may,
like patience, love, and tolerance
each and every day.

Make me a mirror, Lord,
for others then to see,
reflection of the person
that they themselves can be.

Make me a radio, Lord,
a paper or TV,
and use me as a vehicle
to spread the news of thee.

Make me anything, oh Lord,
and I will do the rest.
Make me what you think I need
for I know you know best.

tom catalano

A Glass of Faith

How do we hold it together

and fight the temptation of sin?

How do we do what is right

and not let the devil in?

Why is it sometimes we're stronger

but other times we are weak?

The answer is all in a glass

and whether that glass has a leak.

When you are born you are full

of goodness, of grace, and of love.

You are, in essence, a glass

that's been filled by God up above.

The very nature of glasses

they're fragile but also are strong.

Some people think they won't break

but too late they find they are wrong.   • • •

Cuz glasses don't sit on a shelf

sometimes they'll bump or they'll spill.

And once a glass starts to leak

there's just nothing left there to fill.

A crack can leak all the contents

and also lets other things in.

Like anger, doubt, and frustration,

of course the temptation of sin.

As long as that glass remains full

you'll find you can never go wrong.

Remember to fill up your glass

for a faith that's forever strong.

tom catalano

A Wish

When you wish upon a star

hoping that your dreams go far

instead of gazing way out there

why not turn instead to prayer?

tom catalano

How Close Is That?

The time I almost wrecked the car

or when I stumbled from that bar

    or when I took a beating with a bat.

Just when I thought my luck ran dry

I somehow seemed to just squeak by

    and so I have to ask…how close is that?

The time I almost broke my back

falling from a chimney stack

    or when I had an aching in my gut.

Amazing that I didn't die

I must have been a lucky guy

    I can't believe it…was that close or what?

And when my mother laid in bed

I thought that she was close to dead

    I prayed that God would somehow pull her through.

●●●

He answered every prayer that day

and looking back I'd have to say

    He answered every other one it's true.

Every time that I was down

I never thought He was around

    and I even questioned where He's at.

I can't believe I couldn't see

He'd always been right next to me

    once again I ask…how close is that?

tom catalano

God Is Kind And Merciful

If God is kind and merciful

explain how it could be

that there is death and punishment

throughout our history.

Some look at Noah and the ark,

with animals inside,

and say the flood upon the land

was only 'genocide.'

So why would God, who loves us all,

want everyone to die?

It seems most contradictory

and most hard to deny.

First, let's set the record straight

to fully comprehend,

the measure of a father's love

will not subside or end.

It's just like any parent who

tries teaching right from wrong,   ● ● ●

staying up and worrying

       sometimes the whole night long.

As any parent would admit

       there're rules to be obeyed,

forgiveness gladly given out

       but effort must be made.

But when denial, hate, abound

       with sin and disrespect,

when ages turn their back on God

       well, what do you expect?

They said to God, "Leave me alone,"

       they chose to sin instead.

He pleaded with them to repent

       by then their souls were dead.

When child rejects the father,

       and they refuse to sway,

the recourse must be punishment

       — it is the only way.

The time had come to take a stand

       it broke His heart that day   ● ● ●

to make a sweeping drastic change

with punishment that way.

But sin can't go unpunished

a lesson must be taught,

live with sin and die with sin

— a losing battle fought.

When once again the time had come,

when punishment was due,

God did not punish everyone

his plan was something new.

The world was filled with sinners but

He'd only punish one.

The person who He chose for this

it was His only son.

Jesus bore each person's sin,

was punished for them too,

thereby saving everyone

including me and you.   ● ● ●

For God so loved the world

      that He would send His son,

to die for us and cleanse our soul

      and by His will be done.

If there's any question of

      what God can truly do,

just ask for His forgiveness

      and He'll forgive you too.

So never doubt that God is love,

      He showed us on that day.

You only need invite Him in

      and He'll show you the way.

tom catalano

Guardian Angel

Like an angel Thy spirit's upon me,

with guidance Thy will shall bestow.

A bridge that is not far beyond me,

and Thy love is a net down below.

In darkness I know I'll not stumble,

a touch of Thy hand and I'll see.

I feel I'm blessed with a presence

of an angel whose spirit's on me.

tom catalano

Heaven

"Are there games in Heaven?"

his daughter asked one day.

"Are you allowed to have a pet?

and will God let me play?

When you're dead with your eyes closed

how can you see at all?

Will God help to pick me up

if I should trip and fall?

How come I can't see Heaven

when I look up in the sky?

I don't think I want to go

to Heaven when I die."

The daddy was surprised

and told her, "Hmm, let's see.

I guess that I can tell you

what my daddy said to me.

Heaven is a place where

<u>all</u> your dreams come true   • • •

and you can do most anything

that you want to do.

In Heaven you know everything

you ever need to know.

But only those invited

ever get a chance to go.

You know that God is special

His home is special too.

And when I get to Heaven

I'll be waiting there for you."

"Heaven doesn't sound too bad,"

he heard his daughter say,

"now I think I want to go

— but just not right away!"

tom catalano

Every Morn

Every morn when I awake

as the sunlight starts to break

I have the wherewithal to say,

"Thank you Lord for one more day."

tom catalano

Father and Son

My little boy was nervous

as he came to me one day

and I was not prepared for

what I'd hear him say.

He asked me if I loved him,

of course there is no doubt.

Would I ever send him off?

Now what was this about?

"In Sunday School they told me

that God once had a son,

and He sent Him down to Earth

to help out everyone.

So if God really loved Him

the way they say He did,

why did He let them kill

His one and only kid?

Dad, I know you love me,

I guess it's plain to see,

● ● ●

I just wonder what you'd do

if they came after <u>me</u>."

I didn't know what I could say

to put his mind at ease.

Or even how I'd answer

questions such as these.

I took a breath to fight back

a tidal wave of tears.

I knew that little boy of mine

was wise beyond his years.

"In Sunday School they taught you

of Jesus and the cross.

I like to think of God as

the world's biggest boss.

As any boss will tell you

he's got a job to do.

It matters not how hard the task

you've got to see it through.   • • •

And with any task to do

to make sure it gets done

you send your very best worker

— for God that was His son.

And even though He knew

the price that He would pay,

He gained a billion souls

when Jesus died that way.

I know I'll never have to

send my boy away

all because a father

sent down His son that day.

And so you need not worry

everything will be all right.

Now come and give your father

a hug and kiss goodnight."

tom catalano

I'll Ask The Lord

There're lots of things that I don't know

it's quite a mystery.

But when I die I'll ask the Lord

to explain it all to me.

Like, do you sleep in Heaven?

Does anyone have fun?

And are there really angels

watching out for everyone?

Do we really have free will

or is it all just fate?

Tell me why there's prejudice,

intolerance, and hate.

When we're up in Heaven

can we watch down below,

or do we have to wait for them

when it's <u>their</u> time to go?   • • •

If you created everything

    then who created you?

Are you ever bored, if so,

    then what is it you do?

These things I'll know for certain

    and waiting is just fine.

For I don't think that I want

    to know before my time.

tom catalano

A Father's Prayer

I dreamt I stood before the gate

of bright and brilliant gold.

I felt not healthy, nor infirm,

I felt not young or old.

St. Peter looked at me and said,

"You've lived a life of sin.

I ask you for a reason

why we should let you in."

I stood in awe and trembling,

there's truth in what he said,

but it just does not represent

the life in which I led.

"I've raised my kids in Jesus,

we pray at every meal.

I taught them how to respect life

and never ever steal.

I've taught them to be faithful,

not take His name in vain,

• • •

and if they fail to do some thing

    they're not to pass the blame.

They know they're not to tell a lie,

    I taught them to forgive.

I taught them every living thing

    has a right to live.

I guess the most important thing

    of which I'm proudest of,

is there was not one single day

    that they did not know love.

I know you're right that I have sinned

    in what I've said and done.

You ask me for a reason

    I guess that I have none."

I hung my head most shamefully

    and turned to walk away,

but as I started leaving

    I heard St. Peter say,

"A father's prayer is answered

    when a child calls his name.   • • •

Our relationship with God

is very much the same.

Your children all looked up to you

and you looked up to Him.

And for that He is happy to

forgive you of your sin.

For you I open up the gate

and ask you in to come

to a heavenly reunion

of a Father and His son."

tom catalano

The Big Game
(God Sends In His Son)

At the game the tension was high
　　anticipation filled the air.
Sides were picked and lines were drawn
　　almost everyone was there.

Were we ahead or we behind
　　and how would it finally play out?
"Who would step up to the plate?"
　　those watching began to shout.

Bystanders, fans, and onlookers
　　all craned their necks to see.
Some of them feared the outcome,
　　some said it was destiny.

The coach knew the game's importance
　　it was a critical one.
In spite of some people's objections
　　He sent to the plate His son.　　• • •

His son was a little bit nervous

and wasn't sure He should go.

So before He walked onto the field

there's one thing He had to know.

To His father He did plead,

"I have to beg of you,

if there is no other way

I'll do what you tell me to."

He flung that heavy wooden bat

across His shoulder square.

Every footstep weighed Him down

and was more than He could bear.

He came close to turning back

and slowly looked around,

then stepped upon his laces

and fell down to the ground.　● ● ●

He got up and people laughed
  their mocking laughter hurt.
He lifted up the wooden bat
  covered now with dirt.

As He stood there at the plate,
  and still hurting from the fall,
He knew His father would be proud
  if He could hit the ball.

In just a blur, strike one flew by
  there wasn't much to do.
Then as painful as the first
  He heard them call, "Strike two!"

His knees felt weak and shaky
  His bat felt like a tree.
And just as He expected,
  He heard them call, "Strike three!" ● ● ●

He went back to His father

who hugged Him oh so tight.

His father beamed with pride that day

and said, "You did all right."

His father knew how it would end,

it's more than just a game.

For those who watched that brave young man

will never be the same.

tom catalano

I Do Believe

I do believe 'In God We Trust'

on every currency.

I'm thankful for each cent I have,

He's not forsaken me.

And 'One nation under God,'

is something we should say.

I pledge allegiance and believe

that God made us that way.

To post the Ten Commandments at

a courthouse might be nice.

Perhaps it may just help someone

think of some things twice.

Out on my lawn I want to see

a nativity display.

And if you don't, then you can just

ignore or look away.

• • •

I do believe that it's my right

to worship as I do.

Don't force me to ignore my God

just because _you_ do.

tom catalano

When He Comes Back

Where will I be when it happens?
Cuz happen I know that it will.
I hope He finds that I'm waiting
and yet it worries me still.
Will I be watching a movie?
Will I be watching TV?
Will I be watching a sunrise,
all the time He's watching me?
Will I have my nose in a book?
Will I have my ear to the ground?
Will my mind be focused elsewhere?
Will my eyes be looking around?
Will I still be at the office?
Will I be working at home?
Or will I just be distracted
and chatting away on the phone?
When He comes back for his children
will He find that I hesitate?
Will I be waiting to see Him
or by then will it be too late?

tom catalano

Cornerstone

Call Him a carpenter,

call Him a teacher,

a fisher of men,

or maybe a preacher.

Say what you want

'til the cows come home

— I call Him my cornerstone.

tom catalano

Use Me

Go ahead and use me, Lord.
I am yours to command.
I always want to live for you
and be a helping hand.

I have two eyes to offer Thee
to see beyond my nose.
Show me opportunity
and I will service those.

Two willing ears receive your call,
I pray to hear your voice.
Help me hear the cries of need
and I will help by choice.

One mouth I have to praise your name,
to offer gentle words.
From the dark a candle shines,
I know it's you they heard. •••

I have my heart to offer you,
it's soft, and slightly bruised.
But all my gifts meet open arms.
I know I can be used.

Each day when I begin anew,
you show me where to start.
I'm part of you, and you in me.
I live to share your heart.

emma catalano

I Am A Berry

I am a berry.
Blue berry.
Black berry.
Bruise berry.

My skin is soft
and vulnerable.
Receptive to the
gentlest touch.

I live in the
vineyard of the Lord,
and rest in
my maker's hand.

My maker, the gardener,
is strong and mighty.
He could crush my existence
…but He doesn't.   ● ● ●

He loves me,

in a way I'd never known.

His love is bold and fierce,

and yet...tender.

He cares for

and nurtures me,

providing nutrients and time

for me to grow.

In time, I will mature,

and become a choice wine.

My flavors prepared

to go and serve many.

I will serve the Master,

as He has served me.

He is my vine.

And I am His berry.

emma catalano

Our Spirits Have Soared

This is the time
to remember the love
of our Lord Jesus Christ
who came down from above.

He died on the cross
so that all could be saved.
And now we must follow
the road that He paved.

He taught us to love
everyone on this earth.
He lived without sin
since the time of His birth.

And because we know Him
our spirits have soared.
We find peace in this life
from our friend and our Lord.

emma catalano

A Cross to Bear

It's hard to live our life

as full as God foretold.

We try our best to follow Him

and to the truth we hold.

God said that if we follow Him,

we must take up our cross.

And though we suffer struggles here,

each pain is not a loss.

The yoke we have is heavy,

we crumble by its weight.

God wants us to ask for help

He knows it's not too late.

The pain we suffer in this life

will drive us to the dust.

With tear-filled eyes, we look to Him

— forever God we trust.   ● ● ●

We cannot hold our cross alone,

He wants to share our load.

His footsteps carry all our fears

and leads us on our road.

Out of love He shares the pain.

It's proof to us He cares.

As we walk the path of Christ,

we've all a cross to bear.

emma catalano

All In

Give all that your life has to offer

in your hearts, and words, and deeds.

We are called to be the good soil

when it comes to the sowing of seeds.

God molded your life with a purpose.

He certainly knows you have worth.

We were blessed with the true Holy Spirit

— our own baptism at birth.

The people we see on the street

are really just Jesus disguised.

He knows how we act to the lowly,

how our words have hurt when we lied.

He died on the cross as our shepherd

so that none of His sheep would be lost.

Our sin is a price we must pay

but it was Jesus who balanced the cost. • • •

God gave us all that He had.

His love has freed us from sin.

And that is why we as good Christians

must decide that we are 'all in.'

emma catalano

No Voice

Abortion is wrong, it's just a fact,

and nothing changes unless we act.

Could you kill the boy next door?

That's what the unborn have in store.

Do they have a chance at life

or is it severed by a knife?

Everyone deserves respect,

not just those whom we select.

Love the kids, give them a choice.

Stand up for those who have no voice.

emma catalano

The Heart of Love

I entrust the Lord my heart,
my soul, and mind, and strength.
I have much to thank Him for;
the list is long in length.

The blood of Jesus Christ the Lord
is pumping through my veins.
He leads me toward the joys of life
and helps me through the pains.

My soul resides in Jesus Christ
and He resides in me.
God wrote the blueprint for my soul,
of whom I'm meant to be.

God provides for all I need;
and knowledge I possess.
My goal in life is to achieve
a life of holiness.

● ● ●

It takes a lot of strength sometimes

to make it through the day.

I know God won't abandon me,

and by my side He'll stay.

My God is good and merciful,

and strong, and true, and just.

So that is why the heart of love

is rooted all in trust.

emma catalano

Who You Are

Don't try to 'fit in,'
    but rather, belong.
If you're changing yourself
    then there's something wrong.
God made you as you —
    He loves you as such.
With Him, there's no phrase
    called, "loving too much."
Your life is unique,
    your life's something new.
Your God pays attention
    to all that you do.
In your time of trouble,
    God helps you to thrive.
Therefore, rejoice!
    For you are alive.
It's okay to be different,
    stand out from the crowd.
Don't hide who you are —
    your God is <u>so</u> <u>proud</u>!

emma catalano

Not Forgotten

Gone, but not forgotten,

hidden in the past,

it's sometimes hard to realize

each day is not our last.

The actions that we take

will never go away.

And when we find we've lost our way —

the best thing is to pray.

God knows you are in need,

and <u>your</u> heart He will mend.

To walk you down the road of life —

an angel He will send.

To always care for you,

and always be your friend.

No matter how you suffer here

God loves you 'til the end.   ● ● ●

If you ever think you've lost,

just know that you have won.

For what could be a better prize…

you're seated by God's son!

emma catalano

Repaid

"Gather friends, that we might eat
this feast of living bread.
I will not always be with you,
remember what I've said.

So take my blood and body,
they save you from your sin.
I must die and rise again,
to save my Father's kin.

Come to the Mount of Olives;
come with me to pray.
You know that I must suffer,
it is the only way.

Abba, Father! Hear my cries!
I fear the deed to come.
Though the crowd will question me,
they know not where I'm from. ● ● ●

Abba, Father! Hear my voice!

My soul is troubled still.

Let this cup be passed from me —

yet I will do your will.

Abba, Father! Hear my prayer!

I know the time is near.

Help me through my time of need.

It's pain, not death, I fear.

Peter — when the rooster crows,

it's me you will deny.

When you're asked, you will convince

three others of this lie.

The reason I endure this pain,

is that I love you all.

God wants me to lift you up

— through sin you shall not fall.   • • •

Here is Judas and the priests,

it's me he will betray.

All my peace I give to you,

for I must go away.

Pilate finds no guilt in me

— he wants to let me go.

The crowd, however, won't give up.

They want my death, I know.

So I am nailed to the cross

through pain and agony.

After that, I'm lifted up

so everyone can see.

I see my mother watching me,

and tears roll down her face.

I know that I am leaving Earth

a slightly better place.   ● ● ●

I hand to God my spirit,

so that your will be done."

With one last breath He ended

the Passion of the Son.

So unto Jesus Christ, the Lord,

our sins are ever laid.

Out of love He died for us —

our debts have been repaid.

emma catalano

My Castle of Stone

Open the doors, Lord,
to my castle of stone.
I've been hurt by so many
that I prefer life alone.

Please enter the foyer
of Facebook and lies.
Where I lie through my teeth,
and I shield my eyes.

Not many others
dare go further than this.
So we sit quite content
with our ignorant bliss.

We press on to the kitchen.
I'm comfortable here.
It's here I create,
and I might share my fear.

I fear pain, unimportance,
the death of a friend.
The sweet saddened moment
that all things must end.

● ● ●

Still here and no judgement?
Which moves me to lead
inward yet to my bedroom —
I confess what I need.

I need courage and strength
and a path that is mine.
I need a short fleeting glance
of my Savior divine.

We proceed to the basement.
I pause, hand on the knob.
"I'm scared to go further."
And turning, I sob.

"I've never let anyone
down into this place.
In here are my demons,
that show my true face.

In here are my cobwebs
and bad choices I've made.
Regrets and my mem'ries
that refuse yet to fade."

● ● ●

He retrieved from His pocket
a gold key, as I'd feared.
But as key touched the door,
the whole door disappeared.

"My dear, I knew of this door
and what your demons would be.
But I died for your sins,
and have thus, set you free.

I willed you to show me
each room in your time.
I was love and was patient,
so you knew you were mine."

"Enter oh Lord into
my sanctuary.
You reside in my heart,
which each day, I will carry."

emma catalano

A Child's Christmas

I woke one day and chanced to see

the living room had grown a tree!

As if that was not strange enough

Mom and Dad kept adding stuff.

Like colored balls and lots of lights

and shiny rope that twinkled bright.

Beneath the tree they put a house

with people smaller than a mouse.

Some of them were on one knee

— one was a baby just like me.

Baby Jesus was his name,

and as my parents would explain,

that every year on Christmas morn

we celebrate that He was born.

We give gifts and drink a toast

with people who we love the most.

So on your birthday I will say,

"Jesus, have a happy day!"

tom catalano

The Night Before Jesus

The night before Jesus
and out on the road
to follow a path
for which they were told.

They weathered the wind
and weathered the sand
hoping that someday
they'd understand.

They made the long journey
without much to say.
At night they would take
to their knees and then pray.

They asked the good Lord
why she was the one
to be lucky enough
to deliver His son.

● ● ●

They wanted for hunger,
they wanted for thirst,
but there was a baby
they had to have first.

The time it drew near
— no place to bed down.
The inn was all full
with no more in town.

Thinking they'd have to
bed down on the street,
they looked around back
for a place they could sleep.

'Round back was a stable
— they opened the door.
There was a manger
with straw on the floor.

The animals who
were there for the night,
didn't much mind
this unusual sight.   ● ● ●

He pulled an old blanket
in which he then spread,
for this was to be
a maternity bed.

They huddled together
so they could stay warm.
And then before long
a child was born.

Soon travelers came
with gifts they would bring.
A tribute they said
for the child who'll be king.

For the world this king's birth
holds the promise of joy.
But on this special night
he's just their little boy.

tom catalano

God's Gift

I know you see the ads
        for games and toys galore.
Ideas come aplenty
        when you go to the store.
They all like to tell you
        in stores and on TV
that if you bought this toy
        how happy you would be.
So put them on your list
        with hopes that you'll receive
all the joy they promise
        — if only you believe.
But just don't you forget,
        with all those things you see,
that Christmas is much more than
        some gifts beneath a tree.
Yes, it's fun to hope for
        a brand new shiny toy,
but someday you will learn
        a special Christmas joy.
For then you'll understand
        what everybody knows —
the gift God gives at Christmas
        isn't wrapped in bows.

tom catalano

71

Christmas Upon Us

When Christmas is upon us

and smiles are ear-to ear,

we like to think of all the things

that bring us Christmas cheer.

This year instead of thinking

of all the things we've got,

let's not think what Christmas <u>is</u>

but rather what it's <u>not</u>.

It isn't sugared cookies

or a decorated tree

or presents wrapped and hidden

so no one else will see.

It's not sending greeting cards

with sentimental wishes,

it's not candy in a sock,

or exotic ethnic dishes.

It's not lights and tinsel

draped along the wall;   • • •

all these things are very nice

…but not Christmas at all.

Sometimes we fail to recognize

what truly is at stake —

we just enjoy the frosting

and forget about the cake.

tom catalano

The Wish List

Little Katie sat alone

just making out her list.

She even checked the catalog

to see what she had missed.

There were <u>oh</u> so many toys

that filled up every page,

things for every boy and girl

no matter what their age.

She'd take the list to Santa

and maybe she'd receive

all the presents on her list

when he came Christmas Eve.

A bike, a ball, and some new clothes,

some crayons, and a pet.

A book, a puzzle, and a game,

whatever she could get.

Her mother took her to the mall

and Santa she would meet,   ● ● ●

and sitting in a velvet chair

was Santa in his seat.

The line was long, she'd have to wait,

excitement filled the air.

She could almost read the mind

of every child there.

There was a boy behind her

just standing with his dad.

And what she overheard them say

made her very sad.

"Don't ask Santa for a lot,"

the father told his son.

"If Santa brings us presents

he'll likely just bring <u>one</u>."

The boy just told his daddy,

"I won't make a fuss.

I know that we don't have a lot

at least we still got us."   ● ● ●

When Katie sat on Santa's lap

    she whispered in his ear.

She whispered very quietly

    so no one else would hear.

Then Santa took her list and smiled

    and sent her on her way.

Her mother couldn't wait to hear

    what Katie had to say.

"I think that Santa's going to get

    me what I want this year.

I just hope that he recalls

    what I whispered in his ear.

When I gave my list to him

    I said I think it's fine

if he gives what's on the list

    to the boy who's next in line."

tom catalano

What I Want For Christmas

I've looked through all the catalogs,

I've gone down to the store.

There's a lot of stuff to buy

but I want something more.

The thing I want to have this year

is not found on the shelf,

it's not taken from a rack

and not just for myself.

There're no colors to be matched

or prizes to be won,

and sizes aren't an issue

for it fits everyone.

The gift that I would like to get

will complement His birth.

The gift that I'll be praying for

is lasting peace on Earth.

tom catalano

The Innkeeper

When they came to my front door
    there was not much to say.
Every room I had was full
    — they'd have to go away.

The man seemed weak and weary,
    his feet were sandal sore.
His wife, upon a burro,
    seemed that way and more.

She looked to be with child,
    I sensed she was concerned.
They'd been to every other inn
    and then to mine they turned.

With pleading eyes he touched my arm
    and asked with all his might,
was there not one single room
    where they could spend the night? ● ● ●

In all my years of running
       an inn I've seen a lot
of the poor who want a room
       with money they ain't got.

He seemed just like the others,
       but I could not ignore
the woman on a burro
       and the man beside my door.

I had no room to give them
       although I wish I had,
the longer that I saw her
       the more it made me sad.

As they started leaving
       I called them back and said,
"I don't know why I'm doing this
       but you can take _my_ bed."   • • •

He paused and then he smiled,

    "Sir, you're much too kind.

Thank you for your offer,

    but I'm sure my wife would mind."

I knew I had to help them,

    although I felt not able.

Then I thought about out back,

    what about the stable?!

He offered then to pay me,

    but I would not accept.

I showed them where the stable was

    and that is where they slept.

Early the next morning,

    a child had been born them.

I told them God had blessed her

    and she just said, "Amen."   • • •

Then people started coming

    from near and from afar.

Some of them even said that

    they were following a star.

I dare not speculate on

    who the child might be.

All I know is what His birth

    has gone and done for me.

I no longer turn away

    people from this inn,

for you never know just where

    a new life might begin.

tom catalano

The Gift Tag Tree

It was just a simple thing
>this tag upon a tree,
standing in a vestibule
>for everyone to see.
Upon each tag was written
>a boy or girl's name
for people then to purchase
>some clothing or a game.
Christmas can be difficult,
>some people just get by,
they find it hard to get ahead
>no matter how they try.
Fancy gifts on Christmas morn
>are just a wishful thought,
there's little hope of seeing
>any gifts that Santa brought.　●●●

Every time a tag is pulled

    a child gets to say

someone somewhere helped to make

    a special Christmas day.

No more wishful thoughts this year

    for we will finally see

a gift of love and sharing

    underneath <u>our</u> Christmas tree.

tom catalano

Holiday Blues

I've time off from work
    I haven't a care,
I've finished my shopping
    with money to spare.
But something is wrong
    as I sit by my tree,
I'm sensing a feeling
    I've not felt in me.
I should be happy
    but something's amiss
— it's Christmas and I
    shouldn't feel like this.
I've got many things
    — too much I suppose,
a car and a house
    and a set of new clothes.
I'm saddened to think
    of those with no shoes,
no wonder I'm filled
    with these holiday blues.   ● ● ●

How can I truly

    enjoy what I've got

knowing how many

    of those who have not?

Could it be that I feel

    a wee bit of guilt

while I try to enjoy

    the holiday lilt?

I wish that I could

    think of something to say,

should I make a donation

    or should I just pray?

Whatever I do

    I think I'd best start

to replace this void

    I feel in my heart.

There's one thing I know

    as I'm searching for bliss —

it's Christmas, so maybe

    I <u>should</u> feel like this.

tom catalano

85

The Mission

I've huddled in some doorways
or in the local park,
anywhere to beat the cold
that creeps in after dark.

I've had a job and a house,
a wife and family.
Now there's just a grocery cart
that's never far from me.

I fell upon some hard times
on this I will not dwell.
My life is now a struggle
but mostly I am well.

The winter wind is blowing
and soon there will be snow.
The Mission will be open
and that is where I'll go.

● ● ●

I went 'cross town and stood there,
outside that wooden door,
along with all the others —
some thirty-five or more.

There is only so much room
they like to tell us all.
Twenty beds in the 'Big' room
and five more in the hall.

I was very fortunate
to have a bed that night.
You force yourself not to think
of others and their plight.

Sister Anna greeted us
and handed us some sheets
— something that we did without
when sleeping on the streets.

A Christmas tree was set up,
it was that time of year.
The Father went around and
he wished us Christmas cheer. • • •

He said a little blessing
then served some soup and bread.
I was thankful for the meal,
the warmth, and for the bed.

The soup was chicken noodle
like mother used to make.
The bread was warm and tasty
like sister used to bake.

I drank down all my coffee
and heard somebody say
tonight was Christmas Eve
— tomorrow Christmas Day.

It made me think of Christmas
when I was just a boy.
I would pray for months on end
for that special toy.

The wishing and the hoping
were all part of the fun.
As for pressures of the world
I'm thankful there were none.   ● ● ●

I tried to do the same for
my kids on Christmas Day.
Sadly, I knew early on
it wouldn't be that way.

The Father said that Santa
would visit very soon.
That's all it took to feel
excitement fill the room.

And then the door did open,
just as the Father said.
There stood before us 'Santa,'
white beard and dressed in red.

We all started lining up
to see what Santa's got.
I couldn't help but notice
three people who did not.

A young man and his family
were huddled by the wall.
It surprised me that I hadn't
noticed them at all.

● ● ●

They had a little baby
who slept upon their lap.
They all looked like they could use
a two or three day nap.

I went to go and tell him
that he should get in line.
When 'Santa' reaches in his bag
you don't know what you'll find.

He said it didn't matter
it was nice to be inside.
I didn't try and push it,
yes, at least I tried.

But as I saw that baby,
with cheeks all rosy red,
I did not join the others
I stayed with <u>them</u> instead.

"I know what you are going through,"
I said, "I have no home.
My wife and kids have left me
and now I'm all alone."   ● ● ●

He smiled most disarmingly
and said to have a seat…
they always had a moment
for "friends" that they should meet.

I looked around to be sure
that no one else could see,
and gave him twenty dollars
I was saving just for me.

He said he'd take no charity.
I said that he should try.
"As one friend to another —
you need it more than I."

He reached out and shook my hand
and then I felt all right.
Then someone started singing
my favorite — Silent Night.

As Santa now was leaving
he waved his last good-byes,
and for some unknown reason
tears filled up my eyes.   • • •

Then Father came and asked me
if I would be okay.
I only nodded to him
not knowing what to say.

"You did not join the others
to get a little treat."
I said that I was helping them
get back up on their feet.

I turned to show the priest
the family by the wall
but much to my amazement
I saw no one at all.

Father did not analyze
or say I'd never met,
"Perhaps you got a present
the others didn't get."

He handed me an envelope,
for what I did not know.
"Santa left this here for you
before he had to go."

● ● ●

When I pulled the contents out
it gave me such a thrill.
I just could not believe my eyes
— a twenty dollar bill!

I think about that family
over by the wall,
and how they made my Christmas
the best one of them all.

tom catalano

On His Birthday

Thank you for this food we eat,

but more than that we pray;

thank you for the sunrise

that precedes our every day.

Thank you for the sunset

when every day is done,

but most of all we thank you

for sending us your Son.

tom catalano

The Point

What's the point of Christmas

and sending Christmas cards,

and putting up a tree

and reindeer in the yards?

What's the point of Christmas

and angels in the snow,

holly, presents, eggnog,

and under mistletoe?

Here's the point of Christmas

— the birthday of our king.

Because without whom Christmas

just wouldn't mean a thing.

tom catalano

OTHER BOOKS BY TOM CATALANO:

- **Poetry 'N Motion** - Rhyming poems to make you laugh, tug at your heartstrings, lighten your day, and entertain you. Includes Christmas poems. Favorites include *Hapless Handyman, Golfer's Lament, Beside Me All The Way*, and *Christmas With Dad*. 96 pgs. **$9.95** (ISBN 978-1-882646-03-6)

- **Verse Things First** - Rhyming poems to tickle your funny bone (*Coffee Crutch, Wiseacre Novelty Park*), touch you (*First Love, For You*), and inspire you (*The Brace, The Mission*). Many poems about Christmas. Very popular. As seen on TV! 96 pgs. **$9.95** (ISBN 978-1-882646-43-2)

- **Rhyme & Reason** - The author's first book. Funny, sentimental, and inquisitive rhyming poems on many subjects and emotions. Includes *A Child's Christmas, Work Dreams, Las Vegas Vacation of Mine, The Final Reunion, To Love Is*, and *Pearanoid*. 96 pgs. **$9.95** (ISBN -978-1-882646-07-4)

- **Rhymes For Kids!** - Easy to read rhyming poems that kids K-4+ can enjoy. Promotes friendship (*My Friend Mary-Jean*), caring (*All God's Critters*), being silly (*I Wish I Was a Pizza*), more. 48 pgs. **$6.95** (ISBN 978-1-882646-05-0)

- **Rhymes For Teens** - Rhyming poems that will have pre-teens, teens, and adults smiling, reflecting, and feeling sentimental. Includes *I Survived Elementary School, Stinky Feet, Me Me Me, I Drempt I Was You*, and the patriotic *9-11-01*. 80 pgs. **$9.95** (ISBN 978-1-882646-48-7)

- **I Dig Mud & Yellow Blood** - Funny and touching poems about Caterpillar Inc., their dealers, and users of their products. Includes *Caterpillar-Speak*. Who would have thought the construction and farming industries were so funny? 48 pgs. **$6.95** (ISBN 978-1-882646-91-3)

- **Tall Tales & Short Stories** - 13 short stories of mystery and imagination. Many in the urban fantasy style of Twilight Zone. Illustrated. Favorites includes *Something's In The Basement, Widowmaker, Telephone Madness, The Big 'L,'* and *The Carrier*. 176 pgs. **$10.95** (ISBN 978-1-882646-16-6)

Available through Amazon or contact us:
catalano.tom@gmail.com